Lindfield

Remembered

'MUS' PENFOLDS' A·B·C OF LINDFIELD

A be the Ancient Church of the people,
B be the bells that rings in the steeple.
C be the Common where cricketers play,
D be the ducks in the pond on the way.
E be the eggs in the nestes we spies,
F be the fair an' the cocoanut shies.
G be the grass plots tidy and neat,
H be the high trees that shadders the street.
I be the ins and the outs of the places,
J be the jokes and the jobs that we faces.
K be "King Edward's Memory Hall,"
L be the lectures, an' concerts, an' ball.
M be the mill and the miller a-grindin',
N be the neighbours an' gossip a-findin'
O be "Ol Place" an' the ol'-fashion houses,
P be "Pax Hill" an' pastures where cows is.
Q be the quires that sings in the churches,
R be the river with trouts an' the perches.
S be the signboards that swing in the wind,
T be Town Hill where the houses begin.
U be the uplands for ketching the breeze,
V be the views of the hollers an' trees.
W for waits that shivers and sings,
X be the Xmas tidin's they brings.
Y be the yield of the crops in the season,
Z to be sure there be nothin' in reason.

S.B. Publications

Lindfield Within Living Memory (1995)
also by Gwyn Mansfield and Claudia Gaukroger

First published in 2002 by S.B. Publications
19 Grove Road, Seaford, East Sussex. BN25 1TP

ISBN 1 85770 249 2

Designed and Typeset by EH Graphics (01273) 515527
Printed by Page Turn Ltd. (01273) 821500

Francis Frith and Raphael Tuck are two names that spring to mind of those photographers who, more
than most, recorded scenes and activities throughout the country in the early days of the camera.

In Mid-Sussex we were fortunate to have the similar talents and enthusiasm of Charles Clarke, Harry
Tullett, Douglas Miller, and more particularly as far as Lindfield is concerned, William Marchant, who for
many years viewed every aspect of Lindfield life through his lens, and many examples of his work are
included in this book.

A rare copy of one of his trade cards is illustrated above.

✑ INTRODUCTION ✑

Lindfield has been described, variously, as 'timeless' and 'the jewel in the Sussex crown'.

Timeless might be a slight exaggeration, although the reader perusing this collection of old postcards and photographs of Lindfield might be excused from thinking otherwise. A closer study will often reveal features that differ from that viewed at the present time, some more subtle than others.

Space considerations dictated the number of photographs that could be accommodated and made selection a long but interesting challenge to present a pictorial cross section of Lindfield past. The alternative would have been a much larger volume, or perhaps a second edition.

Old Place, Pretty Corner, Barnlands, the pond, are just a few of the vistas favoured by artists and photographers, and the number and variety of views from which to choose would be sufficient to fill a book. Many of these had previously been published in one form or another but it would be inconceivable not to include at least token photographs representing these familiar views. Less familiar will be many photographs that have never previously been published but which we hope will be fondly remembered by many of our resident readers of long-standing. Consideration has also been given to the many newer residents who have chosen to live in this lovely village, denied the memory aspect of this book, but nevertheless have an interest in how Lindfield once looked and behaved.

Of necessity this album is not complete, but we hope that the pictures that we have personally chosen will please and interest the readers.

Peter Duncan ✦ Gwyn Mansfield ✦ Brian Tester

The photographs on these two pages introduce the views approaching Lindfield from the four points of the compass as our forebears must have seen them. From the North, Town Hill must have been quite a drag for this horse at the end of the delivery round.

Entering from the South at Scrase Bridge, an almost houseless West Common stretched ahead. At the junction with Summerhill Lane, a finger post and a solitary telegraph pole are the only evidence of street furniture.

From the East, Lewes Road is bounded on the left with a line of trees on the Common. In October 1987, hurricane force winds struck southern England and several of these by now mature trees, were brought down.

Smalls Green Cross marks the Western boundary of Lindfield. In more placid times it would have been safe to cross at this major junction to post a letter, not so today.

Built in 1872, Beckworth was the home of Mr Churcher, a well respected authority on growing gladioli. It became a temporary home for evacuee children in 1939, and then in 1977 the W.S.C.C. Divisional Education Office. It was demolished in 1999/2000 to allow the unification of the Junior and Infants' Schools.

Milton House on Black Hill was built in 1850, since then it has experienced several transformations alternating between one or two residences. To the left can be seen the William Allen School of Industry opened by the Earl of Chichester in 1825.

Dr. Alban was a familiar figure going about his rounds driven by Frank Walder in his pony and trap.

When Dr. Alban bought his new 1909 Renault AX two seater, it was the first privately owned motor car in the village. Here the doctor stands proudly beside his vehicle with Mr Walder now promoted to chauffeur.

Named to commemorate the visit to Old Place by His Majesty, the King Edward Hall was built to the design of Mr Walter Tower on land donated by Mr W.A. Sturdy at a total cost of just over £2000, raised by public subscription. It was declared open on 11th January 1911 by Lt.Col. Dudley Samson who, after reciting a thirteen verse poem composed by himself in honour of the occasion, drew attention to the date being a rare palindrome of 11.1.11.

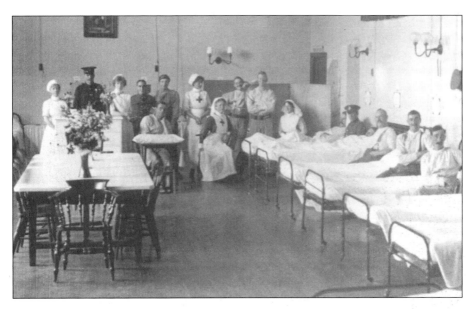

During the First World War the Red Cross, with many local volunteers, transformed King Edward Hall into a convalescent hospital for wounded troops returning from the fighting on the Western Front. On sunny days, a bright striped awning would be erected with seats set out to allow the men to relax and enjoy the vista of the pond, relax, and try to forget their horrendous experiences.

The present United Reformed Church dates from 1857/58, replacing a Chapel on the same site, built in 1811. This early photograph was taken at a time when the church had two main entrance doors, which subsequently were replaced with a single centrally placed entrance.

Ryecroft was first acquired as a Manse in 1888 and was used for many years until the costs of upkeep were considered too expensive. Other houses in the village were used to accommodate ministers and Ryecroft was then sold in 1953, only to be re-purchased in 1983 to resume the role of Manse.

The first recorded incumbent of All Saints Church was William de Bosco in 1230. The architecture and siting of this lovely church have made this a favourite subject for artists and photographers.

The Rev. Francis Sewell spent much of his personal fortune restoring All Saints Church and built the Mission opposite as a school, later to become The Sewell Memorial Mission, now converted to private houses. The Mission ultimately moved to Chaloner Road and subsequently was renamed The Evangelical Free Church.

A very early view across the pond that dates prior to 1870. This was about the time that Amon Anscombe built Eldon Lodge as a wedding present for his son, Parker.

This picture was taken from the cover of Miss Helena Hall's book *Lindfield Past and Present* proving that these quiet waters did once have a functional use. Legend has it that stage coaches would drive through the pond to cool their wheels.

A fall of snow will invariably give a completely different perspective to a familiar scene. In less regulated times when the pond froze, it acted as a magnet to those brave and hardy enough to take to the ice.

This photograph was taken when the motor car was still in relative infancy. Mr Martin must have had confidence to invest in this mode of transport, his style of advertising, though, would not be tolerated today. The car in the foreground bears a Southport registration PY407 issued in late 1923, and the car appearing out of the garage c1903 a lateral radiator Renault.

❧ THE HIGH STREET ❧

Tinker, tailor, candlestick maker, in its time shops and traders plied their business throughout the length of the High Street in such profusion and variety that it was hardly necessary to travel further afield. Leading were the three department or variety stores, a brewery, butchers who had their own slaughter houses, grocers, greengrocers and fruiterers, milliners, tailors, provision merchants, ironmongers, corn chandlers, newsagents, watchmakers, haberdashers, fishmongers, drapers, chemists, bakers, shoe makers, hairdressers, florist, bookseller, library, antiques, stationers, toys, wine merchants, saddlers, confectioners, coal and coke merchants, undertakers, and agencies for insurance.

Some of these remain, even retaining the earlier name, many have gone and have been converted to desirable dwellings, although in some instances a close scrutiny will reveal the outline of the former shop front.

The next few pages are devoted to some of those shop premises.

1689 is the date over the front door of Bay Pond Cottage, sited on the edge of the common and facing the pond. This photograph was taken about 200 years later when the sign heralded the business of Henry Best, general carrier, coal and coke merchant.

John Anscombe founded the family business of contractors, ironmongers and undertakers in 1820. He was succeeded by his son, Amon, who proceeded to expand by building workshops in Pond Croft Road and the builders merchants' shop on the corner.

The village store of Gosling & Uridge was later to become Masters. Following the transfer of the business Mr Uridge retained the post office franchise working from a small room in the same building. He relinquished his post office role on the marriage of his daughter to Mr Chandler, and the newly weds moved to the present P.O. location where Mr Chandler was sub-postmaster for 45 years.

There are many fond memories of Master's Department Store which opened in 1864. From that time until it closed one hundred years later, this family business could clothe, feed, furnish, insure, and ultimately bury residents of the village and beyond.

The family name of Box has been synonymous with Lindfield trade over many decades. The family owned market gardens and nurseries to the east of the High Street that extended to The Bent Arms and Luxford Road, as well as grazing pastures for their livestock. This enabled them to sell their own meat and produce from these two High Street shops. Despite changes in ownership, the shops have changed very little over the intervening years. The top photograph has Mr and Mrs Box with their staff posing in front of the giant black poplar tree, a village landmark until it had to be felled in 1962.

Durrant is a name that has been prominent in Lindfield since 1790 or thereabouts. Thomas concentrated his skills in running a very successful piano factory, but it was Edward who was more diverse with his entrepreneurial talents, owning the brewery, the fascia board to which is about the limit of photographs of this local industry. The shop was an Aladdin's cave, offering among other items, drapery, groceries, glass and fine china. Living 'over the shop', Mr and Mrs Durrant are pictured outside their front door. Lindfield rejoices in some splendid honorary titles, such as Harbour Master. Mr Durrant enjoyed the epithet of Mr Wattle, in response to undertaking to store the sheep fencing between fairs.

The Linden Tree, as it is now known, offers comfort and a warm welcome, this was not always so. As part of Mr Durrant's brewery it was appropriately called The Stand Up Inn. A total absence of any form of seating was intended to deter his workmen from dallying in supping their ale.

The old forge in Denmans Lane was part of the brewery and was worked for over sixty years by John Sharman, and later his apprentice, George Brown. The regular trade of horses requiring to be shod was a popular free show for children who were permitted to watch from the doorway.

The Postal Services in Lindfield initially had a nomadic lifestyle, moving to different addresses in the High Street, but it has been on the present site since the mid-19th century. Photographs are uncannily rare and this is the earliest that could be traced, taken by author S.P.B. Mais in 1965.

In 1910, Barclays Bank opened for business on Thursdays only from a single room in one of these cottages. The bank bought the freeholds in 1929 and started to introduce a more frequent and extensive banking service. This all came to an end in 1999 when the big High Street banks decided to curtail their rural offices, with the result that Lindfield suffered a double blow, losing both Barclays and Lloyds within a day of each other.

Bespoke tailoring, including providing the liveries for servants employed in the surrounding mansions, was the speciality of Mr Kimber, but this photograph gave no indication of when or where he employed his expertise. Fortunately the 1881 Census provided the answers - 4 Albert Terrace, now The Birman Gallery.

The small shop window of Mr William Mighall's sweet shop was big enough to attract children pressing their noses against the panes of glass, relishing the selection of goodies inside. His son, Harold, succeeded to the business and on his retirement the property was taken over by Bob Lamberts T.V and radio shop, and is now The Coffee Connection.

This photograph is a favourite and often-seen early illustration of Lindfield High Street showing the newsagent, stationery and gift shop owned by Miss Simmons and her friend, Miss Price. Outside, down the unmade road, a drover urges his flock on their way to pastures new.

Mr Joseph Pranklin standing outside the boot and shoe shop which he founded in 1859. The business passed through the female line of the family until 1966, but the trade name remains.

Once a farmhouse, built in the 14th century, a bakery has stood on this site since 1796. In 1871, Mr Smith, the baker at that time, took on young Richard Humphrey as assistant. Four short years later, Richard was able to acquire the business and proudly display his name over the shop front. He died in 1940, aged 85, having served the village as baker for 55 years, but even after all these years the Humphrey name has been retained by subsequent owners. Deliveries were made well beyond the village environs by horse drawn van, on the back of which was the painted invitation to 'try a free sample of wholemeal bread'.

Adjacent to the Red Lion car park is now the shop of David Adam, but over the years the property has had many different identities. In this view it was owned by Mr Wearn who, apart from the range of Spratt's animal feeds advertised on the end wall, also styled himself as a grocer, draper, hosier, stationer etc. The lombardy poplar tree opposite fronted the Poplar Hand Laundry.

The proprietor of this High Street grocers, believed to be where Eve's Tea Room, Past and Present is now situated, stands behind his well stocked counter, ready to give the personal service and attention to customers that was expected at the time. The shop is packed with a wonderful array of mouth-watering delicacies, and a thoughtful chair is placed for the comfort of the customers while they await their purchases to be weighed and wrapped.

A hundred years after being designated Victoria Terrace, this row of shops to the west side of the High Street, and Albert Terrace opposite, are hardly remembered as such, having been renumbered as part of the High Street.

Bert Crosley initially had his greencrocery in the Well House, part of Barnlands, before moving to larger premises in Victoria Terrace. At the time of this photograph properties in the High Street had not been numbered, but the ornamental corbel, an architectural feature, confirms that the address was 69 High Street.

Upwey, Caldicote and The Limes are now three private houses situated in the High Street just north of Hickmans Lane. Before they were converted to this use, the three properties were combined to provide another Lindfield department store, owned in turn by Mr Wratten and Mr Funnell. As can be seen from the lower photograph, taken during Mr Wratten's occupancy, space was at a premium and the interior resembled an Aladdin's cave with a remarkable display of household goods. Weather permitting, it was not unusual for stalls to be set up on the grass verge outside.

Recent refurbishment of Spongs has been sympathetic to its earlier style and usage. Opposite, at least two of these houses also had a commercial past. Mr Bish made gaiters and gloves in Viking Cottage, and in the 1930s it was a lending library. Seckhams, when occupied by Miss Louisa Cuppage, and several cats, offered curios under the heading of 'Many Cargoes'.

Mr Clifford Featherstone was a clocksmith, probably the last of several that once served Lindfield. He was largely responsible for the installation of the north dial on All Saints Church. Next door, can be seen the extended shop front of Mr Charman's bakery.

Once this part of the High Street contained many shops. Osborne Cottage many years ago, for a short period, had been the Post Office. Welfares nearby was the newsagent, and Mr Driver sold wet fish from Crosskeys.

Many will miss No. 1 Albert Terrace which was occupied by Mr Alex Shepherd. Ironmongery, hardware and corn chandlery were his stock in trade, and apart from the useful service the shop provided it had the added attraction of the pungent aromas that wafted around inside.

Barnlands is one of the most picturesque and oldest properties in Lindfield. At the time of this photograph Messrs Holman and Crosley were side by side in competition. Miss Maud Savill was responsible for restoring the building to residential use.

This is an interesting panoramic view looking up High Street with Master's Store on the left and Box's on the right. An additional point of interest is the siting of the monster 70ft high telegraph pole. When these were erected by the Post Office in the early 1900s, there were inevitable objections. The authorities listened with some sympathy to that which had to be erected in All Saints churchyard and made concessions of shape and colour, but they drew the line when similar concessions were expected elsewhere. Ultimately they conceded that the one in this photograph could be adorned with a weather vane, provided that the cost and maintenance was the responsibility of the village.

Evidence of more shops extending to the top of the High Street. With the exception of the antique shop of Spongs those north of Dukes Road have now gone.

Now reverted to the earlier name of Marlowe House, Aramintas was one of the favourite rendezvous for morning coffee and afternoon teas, especially in the summer months when, weather permitting, it was a delightful place to linger in the well-laid-out gardens.

Judging from the display of meat and game suspended in the shop window, Lindfield residents were spoilt for choice from Mr Wickham's butchery shop. The Model 'T' Ford van suggests that this photograph was taken in about 1924.

Before Mr Wickham acquired the butchery business at the top end of the High Street it was owned by Mr Jenner. The weatherboarded building alongside is thought to have been the slaughterhouse. Demolished, the space has been filled with Tallow Cottage, the only newly built house in Lindfield High Street since 1945.

Both these photographs show the Tiger when, as one wag has put it - it had spirituous rather than spiritual connotations. Next door was The Little Shop run by Mrs Kate Jenner to which choirboys, having sung at a wedding and received their reward, would make a beeline, to deliberate how best to spend their pennies.

To get to a wedding or just from A to B in style and comfort, George Mason was able to oblige with his fly cabs, carriages, waggonettes and landaus. When the hated tollgate was removed he, by common assent, was accorded the honour of having the first free passage, being considered as having paid more tolls than anyone else.

Durrant's shop is open for business. The Stand Up Inn was still called just that, the telephone box of an earlier model unassailed by vandals, the style of the cars suggest maybe the 1920s, and the shadows from the telegraph pole indicate a morning photograph. But where are the people?

❦ PIANOS, CONCERTS AND SKIRTS ❧

The short walk along the sloping footpath from the High Street between the florists and Estate Agents leads to the modern Medical Centre, the Tollgate senior citizens housing and car park with lovingly tended flower beds. This all came about in 1975 when the building, here viewed from the air, had become derelict and no longer had an economic future.

For over 150 years, however, the original building saw many transformations.

In 1840 Mr Thomas Durrant, employing a small band of skilled craftsmen, ran a thriving pianoforte manufacturers, initially for the home market, but recognising that the expatriates and troops leaving to establish the Raj in the Indian sub-continent would appreciate the sound of home entertainment, he applied his entrepreneurial talents to this potential market. This led to a thriving export business and it was not unusual for three or more pianos to be transported at a time by horse and cart to the London docks.

Mr Durrant retired to Rugby in 1881 and put the premises up for sale. There does not appear to have been much interest, and very soon the windows became targets for the catapults of local urchins.

It was round about this time that the possibility of building a village hall was mooted, but the enthusiasm of the proposers was not matched by the villagers. Notwithstanding this lack of interest, Mr Eastwood and a few friends acquired the premises and in a grandly worded announcement in The Mid Sussex Times dated 13th March 1883 announced that

> "The Assembly Rooms, when opened, will form one of the most important features of the village. It will have a spacious and well protected entrance, a staircase of great breadth and solidity leading to the first floor auditorium which will be able to seat 150 to 200 persons. A raised stage at one end will be faced by a gallery at the other, the latter being intended either as private boxes, or cheap sittings, as the occasion demands".

No mention was made that the ground floor would become the centre for Mission Rooms for gospel and temperance work.

The Assembly Rooms did indeed flourish with a packed programme of theatricals, soirees, lectures, exhibitions and recitals. Soon the word was that Lindfield was the Sussex home of entertainment. Charles Dickens and Oscar Wilde both made appearances, and there is more than a hint that Marie Lloyd once graced the stage.

Nearly 24 years after first suggesting and dismissing the advantages of a purpose-built village hall, opinions had changed and on land provided by Mr Sturdy, and to a design by Mr Walter Towers, The King Edward Hall came into being in January 1911. This spelt the end of The Assembly Rooms which, from programmes and press reports, had in its short life been greatly appreciated by villagers.

Not recorded, but certainly strongly rumoured, was that the building lay empty until the First World War when it was, literally, turned into a rabbit warren, producing a regular tasty supply of meat to supplement the rations.

Post war, the building and yard were used for general storage whilst the structure became ever more dilapidated.

After the Second World War, two brothers from Burgess Hill viewed the old Assembly Rooms as possible suitable premises in which to establish their skirt factory. The grand staircase had become a lot less grand, the wind blew through countless holes in the windows and gaps in the buildings ageing fabric, but after a good spring clean and a lick of paint, the brothers had work benches and machines installed. There are many ladies still alive who remember either working there or buying the good quality products direct. The business expanded and contracts for brand names such as Gor-Ray and Slimma were obtained. Keeping up with market trends in the 1950s was essential and the brothers, Paul and Herbert Christian, produced mini and maxi skirts and, with slight diversification, manufactured kilts, dungarees, ladies shorts and blouses.

By the late 1960s the business was facing financial difficulties and finally went into receivership.

The Board School in Lewes Road was opened in 1881 as scheduled, although it will come as no surprise to learn that the builders were still adding the finishing touches. Many older residents in the village speak highly of the standard of education received and the dedication of the teaching staff. Plans for a new school building were long drawn out, but eventually, with the facilities having outlived the standards required for modern education, the building was closed in 2000 and the Junior and Infants' Schools were amalgamated.

These two photographs were taken in a more innocent era, a period when parents had fewer worries of their children having to contend with the lack of chain link fencing around the pond, or having to take one's life in one's hand to cross the road to enjoy the freedom and safety of fun on the Common.

If any views are required to suggest that Lindfield really is timeless, these photographs portray that assumption. Spring Lane, taken over one hundred years ago compares very much with that of today. Manor House Cottage is later, probably about 1920, but from the outside little has changed since then.

High noon - 31st October 1884. Crowds thronged the High Street to witness the permanent removal of the much hated tollgates. More celebrations were to follow when they were consigned to the bonfire celebrations of that year.

Toll dodging would have been a popular pastime but the Newchapel & Brightelston Turnpike Trust were not unaware of this prospect so installed a second tollgate across Hickmans Lane.

The Bent Arms derives its present name from Dr. Bent, a local dignitary, but it had previously been known as Wichelos and The White Lion of Lindfield Town. Conservation rules did not apply when this photograph was taken and it was usual for traders to paint their walls with advertising.

Meets have congregated in Lindfield, but not very often and not for a long time. The last that can be recalled included comedian Jimmy Edwards riding to hounds. This view dates from the 1920/30 era and is of The Old Surrey and Burstow Foxhounds.

This photograph c.1948 of The Bent Arms displays the Bent family crest as the pub sign. Between then and refurbishments made three or four years ago, the Landlord demonstrated a sense of humour by displaying a sign showing a pair of entwined arms, each hand clutching a tankard of ale.

A lighted candle is believed to have caused the fire that nearly destroyed the Bent Arms in 1920. Although the upper floor was gutted, it could have been much worse but for the prompt action by Lindfield Fire Brigade, and in particular Fred Nye.

Ten miles per hour, ten miles per hour! You can repeat it until you are blue in the face, but can any resident recall an instance of this sign being observed.

Froyls in the High Street has a well documented history that dates back to Elizabethan times. The present frontage though is Georgian. Charles Dickens was a regular visitor when the house was owned by his friend, Dr. Richard Tupper.

Cycle supply and repairs was the vocation of Mr Holman in his High Street shop. Cycling was, of course, a popular mode of transport but with the advent of the wireless, the shop was a convenient place to have accumulators recharged, and later a hand operated petrol pump was installed.

The Musical & Literary Institute was situated next to The Bent Arms and later had a second floor added. To its left ran the bridleway known as Brushes Lane leading to Phineus Jupp's forge. The Institute was pulled down in the 1970s to allow access to the newly built Dukes Road, but after protest the first 100 metres was allowed to retain the name Brushes Lane.

The Lindfield pleasure fair in full swing c.1904.

Shepherds in Sussex smocks pen the sheep behind wattle fences at the last fair to be held in the High Street in 1906.

↬ THE LINDFIELD FAIRS ↫

It was in 1344 that King Edward III granted by Royal Charter the right for two fairs to be held annually at Lindfield, or Lindeskeldon as it was known at that time. Like many ancient fairs in rural areas, these were largely for the sale of livestock, and so far as Lindfield was concerned this meant sheep and horses, although tinkers, gypsies and entertainers plied their wares and talents.

The April fair soon passed into history and only the St. James's fair in August survived. With the introduction of Bank Holidays in 1889 a petition was raised to move the designated date of the 4th to the 8th August.

Signs that the fair was imminent were evident two or three days before as drovers blocked roads as they directed their flocks to the High Street where anything up to 20,000 head of sheep would be penned. As traffic increased changes had to be made and in 1906 the livestock fair moved to the common. If the sheep attracted the farmers in great numbers, the pleasure fair proved an even greater allure to the population for many miles around, with the Southdown Bus Company running charabanc excursions to Lindfield. As can be appreciated from the main photograph, the event became huge and amid the deafening haggling and bartering of the farmers, traders and gypsies trying to compete with the clatter of the showmen's engines, the music from several steam organs and the bellowing of the sideshow barkers. Residents would flock to the common, old friendships were renewed as relatives and friends made it a special occasion and for the few days that the August Fair remained, Lindfield made merry.

The main lessee would sub-let plots to other travellers and as a consequence it was not unusual for rides to be duplicated, on one occasion three dodgem tracks competed against each other. Centre of attraction always was Mr Tommy Smith's three abreast gallopers, but just about every other ride in fairground history has graced Lindfield common, big wheel, octopus, chair-o-planes, paratrooper, waltzer, Noah's Ark, Ben Hur, swing boats, wall of death, whilst scattered around were innumerable stalls such as hoop-la, roll-a-penny, striker, rifle range, fishing, darts and more. Around the periphery the sideshows with their gaudy fascias attracted the punters with freak shows, Wild West knife-throwing and fire-eating, and of course the inevitable boxing booth inviting local young men to test their mettle.

During the two World Wars, villagers would keep the Charter in being by setting up a few stalls on the common to sell such trinkets as were available. When the cattle market opened in Haywards Heath, the method of dealing changed from barter to auction and this led to the demise of the Lindfield cattle fair. The pleasure fair was to continue, but tastes have changed and the attractions of theme parks has, in recent years, tended to diminish the importance and attraction of the great days of Lindfield Fair.

Now included in the Conservation Area, Compton Road looks, apart from the parked cars, very much as it does today. There have been suggestions that the top photograph gives the impression that this was not a through road, but this is not so.

Just who was Hickman to justify having the longest road in Lindfield named after him? A theory has been put forward that this was derived from Hackman, but this only repeats the question, who was Hackman? These two photographs, one from the east, the other from the west are of that part of the lane nearest the High Street, and which more often than not was referred to as Side Lane.

The gardens and surrounding land of Finches was immense, requiring the attention of twelve full time gardeners. It also boasted a large aviary of exotic birds which, it is rumoured, were released to the wild at the outbreak of hostilities in 1939. Owned by Mr Walter Savill of Shaw Savill Shipping Line, his daughter, Maud, was responsible for restoring several village properties.

In 1947, the Tudor style mansion of Finches was converted into The County Hotel with accommodation for 100 guests. It soon became the leading venue for weddings, dinners and other social functions, but this all came to an end in 1964 when the whole of Finches estate was developed for private housing.

First impressions are said to be important and this view of Finches Lodge certainly creates a good impression. The Lodge, much enlarged, still has a commanding position at the entrance to the housing estate, but the traffic is now more frenetic.

Built in 1839 as a Vicarage, the Welkin became a private school for boys in 1948 on being derequisitioned by the Army. It was demolished in 1961 for housing development, but the first proposals for 200 flats in five eight-storey blocks caused a local uproar.

Going back to the 14th century, Buxshalls has experienced many different spellings. The Lodge, at the entrance from Ardingly Road, suffered superficial damage from one of the few bombs dropped by the Luftwaffe. The mansion has been home to Lt.Col Dudley Sampson, and local Member of Parliament Sir Henry Cautley, who on ennoblement in 1936 adopted the title Lord Cautley of Lindfield.

With 17 children, dentist Mr L.C. Gibbin needed a big house and so built Great Walstead, here seen in 1946. Auctioned in 1908 with a winning bid from a Sheffield steel millionaire, who died soon after. His widow leased the property to, among others, Lord Riddell who frequently entertained his friend, Prime Minister Lloyd George. In 1927 the parents of Kilvington School, Enfield, were told of the move to Great Walstead.

In about 1550, the Chaloner family moved into Kenwards. It was in 1724 that the Earl of Chichester had most of it pulled down, the materials being transported away to build Stanmer. All that now remains is the converted stable block.

The Deans' Mill house.

The Deans' Mill narrow gauge railway.

ᥰ THE DEANS' MILL ᥱ

The Deans' Mill is the last of 27 water mills that once lined the banks of the River Ouse in Sussex and which were used for grinding corn or in paper manufacture. It is probable that a mill stood on the Deans' Mill site as early as 1761.

The navigation of the River Ouse with 18 locks came about by Act of Parliament in 1790 and in its prime was capable of accommodating barges of 45ft in length and 14ft in width, carrying loads of up to 30 tons. It ran from Lewes to near Balcombe, was dug by hand with mule transport carting away the spoil, taking 22 years to complete. Belgium bricks for the Balcombe railway viaduct were barged up river, but on completion in 1841, railways proved a cheaper form of transport than canal barges.

In 1935 Deans' Mill had been left decaying for 27 years when Mr and Mrs Horsefield bought it and set about renovation. An engineer by profession, Mr Horsefield had a good eye and ability for solving mechanical problems, and in a remarkably short time, by September 1937 in fact, he had the mill back in working order and had their own brand of wholemeal flour on sale around the district. Mrs Horsefield put her vegetarian convictions into practice by opening a meat-free restaurant in Haywards Heath which proved very popular. Next, the old Elizabethan barn was converted to serve afternoon teas on the lawns and as an added attraction, but probably more to satisfy Mr Horsefield's latent engineering aspirations, a narrow gauge railway was laid out to encircle the grounds, offering joy rides between tea and cakes.

Mr Horsefield was not just an enthusiastic engineer, he was an over-enthusiastic train driver and there are reports of mishaps when taking the curves too fast. The traction engines have an interesting history. The first was a wet steam engine which lacked power to negotiate the several gradients around the circuit with a full load of passengers in the open toast rack dolly. This engine was put up for sale in 1938 but it is doubtful if it found a buyer. An American Cagney engine was bought as a replacement and the fate of this is also uncertain. There is a rumour that the Canadian Army, when stationed at Paxhill, offered to carry out repairs, and that was the last seen of it. The last locomotive is that shown in the photograph which finally turned up at Dreamland in Margate, the coachwork modified to give a more streamlined appearance. In very recent years this engine has been given a new lease of life through the restoration by a narrow gauge railway enthusiast.

Milling stopped in 1976 and the mill and barn are now private homes.

Once navigable as far as Balcombe Viaduct, these photographs illustrate the rush of water when the mill gates are opened, while the tranquil waters upstream were a favourite setting for picnics and boating.

May Day 1906 was the first day of the Lindfield Swimming Club and quickly became a favourite among villagers which was to last for thirty years. Situated upstream from Medwyn Bridge, the modesty of the time excluded mixed bathing. Apart from the general frolicking in the water, galas and water polo matches were often held.

The Fire Brigade and the Merryweather Little Gem horse-drawn engine.

The Fire Brigade at first were only equipped with hand carts.

∾ THE LINDFIELD FIRE BRIGADE ∿

In 1899, the Parish Council sanctioned the formation of a local fire brigade of volunteers. Still standing is the original fire station in Lewes Road but now used by the Dramatic Club as a scenery store, but in those early days the brigade kept and maintained their primitive equipment of handcart and leather hoses. A 1904 minute reports that the Fire Captain put his men to the test by heralding a fire drill, despatching the two messengers on foot or by bicycle to raise the alarm, with a satisfactory time lapse between then and the first men on the scene with the emergency handcart of fourteen minutes.

Village blacksmith, John Sharman was Captain, he set about raising funds to purchase a more substantial steam engine, and this resulted in Merryweather 'Little Gem'.

With the amalgamation of the districts under the heading of Cuckfield Urban District Council in 1934, the Lindfield brigade was disbanded. During those 35 years they had attended many haystack blazes, some of which took several hours to bring under control, whilst among the bigger fires tackled was one at Chailey Heritage, and it is generally acknowledged that but for the sterling and prompt action taken by these volunteers in 1920, The Bent Hotel would have been completely destroyed.

The old fire station in Lewes Road had originally been the stables of Pear Tree House, but were brought back into defence service by the Auxiliary Fire Service in the Second World War. At the height of the blitz, these local volunteers were called upon to assist the over-stretched units in Portsmouth to extinguish blazing oil tank installations.

A tuppenny fare would take a villager as far as Haywards Heath on this first motor omnibus, or for another tuppence, all the way to Cuckfield. It was a comfortable ride by all accounts, although those on the top deck were at risk from low overhanging boughs.

This team of postmen are seen leaving Haywards Heath sorting office to start their early morning rounds, those on bicycles being responsible for deliveries to Lindfield and surrounding villages.

Mid Sussex Steam Laundry.

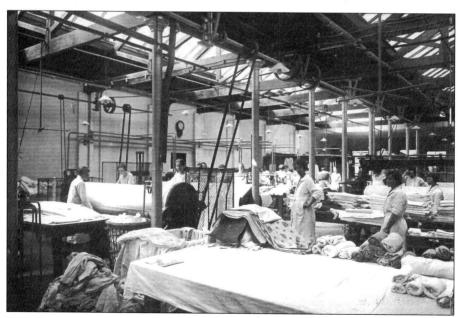

View inside the laundry workrooms.

ᘇᕽ The Mid Sussex Steam Laundry ᕽᘇ

At the turn of the 19th/20th century, a lass becoming pregnant out of wedlock could expect to receive little comfort from her parents in particular or society in general. She had brought shame on the family and was likely as not to be told "never darken this door again". For some the punishment could be much more severe such as being locked in an asylum for many years.

At that time social reformers were in the minority, but locally, The Rt. Hon. Olivia, Dowager Countess of Tankerville, had set about relieving the plight of these unfortunate girls, first by founding a laundry at Wooler in Northumberland, which offered these young single mothers the opportunity of employment, a roof over their head and a situation which did not deprive them of bringing up their offspring.

With this project successfully in operation, she turned her attention to repeating it in Lindfield and mainly through her efforts the Mid Sussex Steam Laundry was built on land at the north end of Gravelye Lane and which opened its doors for business in 1901.

Come Lady Day in 1912, the administration was transferred and entrusted to the Salvation Army. Apart from the necessary functions to operate a working laundry such as receiving, sorting, washing, drying, ironing and return delivery departments, facilities were provided for each girl to have her own bed-sitting room, and a creche was provided for their children when mother was at work.

The laundry continued under the guidance of The Salvation Army until 1922 and from then on was run by a local committee, but after the war it was sold to Mr J. Carter who proceeded to run it as a commercial venture, employing many local ladies irrespective of their maternal needs.

Mr Carter was a resourceful man and found that by rigging up a contraption on the 74ft high chimney, he could capture the escaping steam in glass bottles and was able to sell the distilled water to chemists for the preparation of their medicines and to garages for topping up batteries. If the chimney itself was a local landmark, the hooter mounted high to signify the start and finish of work played a significant part in the village, being so accurate that watches and clocks could be set from its sound.

In 1972 the laundry closed and the site was cleared to make way for Grey Alders housing.

The origin of the name Denmans Lane is uncertain and some have suggested that it might be a corruption of Dead Man. In the late 19th century it was often referred to as Batchelors Lane, after the blacksmith working the forge at that time. Looking from both east and west, these photographs show the weatherboard barn that was where the wattle sheep fences were stored between Fairs.

Batchelors Lane in about 1900 and a view taken along Hickmans Lane showing The Witch Inn, formerly The Bricklayers Arms in the distance.

The Silver Star Orchestra was formed in 1934 and was in regular demand to play at dances, parties, weddings and village 'hops'. It was only with the advent of war in 1939 that the band was disbanded as one by one the members joined H.M. Forces. The Lindfield Harmonica Pirates showed great versatility in their repertoire, often leading parades and accompanying the singing at open-air Church Services. Their dancing engagements included several bookings at Sherry's Ballroom in Brighton.

Lindfield is quite renowned for celebrating Royal occasions. On 12th May 1935 it was time to celebrate the Silver Jubilee of George V. These two photographs are from a series taken by William Marchant. A short time-lapse occurred as he re-focused his camera, bringing different sections of the parade into view. After the choirboys came the men in academic gowns, and then the Harmonica Pirates.

Lindfield takes pride in the celebration of Royal events. The Union flag is always raised outside King Edward Hall on officially designated dates, and Coronations and Jubilees have always been celebrated in great style. In 1911 George V was crowned King and villagers came out to celebrate with flags waving, bands playing and a great deal of marching both up and down the High Street.

The Coronation of George VI on 12th May 1937 was another opportunity for celebration. Central among the many events were the aquatic sports and competitions held on and in the pond, a leading figure being Cambridge rowing blue, the Rev. Sydney Swann. A tableau representing the Imperial Crown was erected on the green opposite with over 100 coloured light bulbs symbolising the jewels.

The original caption on this photograph clearly states Lovers Walk, Lindfield, but that romantic notion has long been forgotten; magnifying the image reveals in the distance Malling Priory confirming that this was a part of a very rural Hickmans Lane.

This is another photograph that at first was difficult to pinpoint for the cottage is no more. After much investigation the conclusion is that the location was on the east side of Town Hill just past Spring Lane.

✦ FIRING THE ANVIL ✦

The old Sussex custom of firing the anvil is still performed but mainly at national and local times of celebration. Village blacksmith, John Sharman, performed this ritual in 1900 to mark the relief of Mafeking and continued the practice year after year and, as these photographs depict, on the occasion of the Coronation of H.M. the Queen in 1953. After Mr Sharman's death, the tradition has been maintained by his watchful apprentice, George Brown. The anvil is turned upside down and the hole in the base is filled with explosive then plugged with a wooden peg which is drilled with a wet gimlet. From a short fuse of gunpowder, ignition is from a hot blacksmith's iron.

Crossways, Sunte Avenue, now a residential retirement, home has been much extended since this photograph was taken but is still easily recognisable.

This photograph had been captioned Station Road, Lindfield which was a mystery waiting to be solved. Fortunately an old map dated 1874 solved the riddle for Sunte Avenue was once the most direct route to Haywards Heath station.

Another view looking along Sunte Avenue providing an idyllic rural setting.

Sunte Avenue around 1930, the lean-to building on the right was then a laundry, before Mr Clough opened the shop there in 1937.

❧ THE LINDFIELD MUSHROOM FACTORY ❧

Around 1935, Mr Frederick Smith was casting his eyes around Lindfield in search of available land for his planned nursery garden. Two plots were on offer, one in Luxford Road belonging to Mr Box which had long been under cultivation, the other was to the rear of Noah's Ark Cottage in Lewes Road, an area prone to regular flooding. Not surprisingly, he chose the former.

Coincidentally about the same time a Canadian gentleman, Mr A. Slack, nursed ambitions to grow mushrooms on a commercial scale and was also on the lookout for a suitable plot. Being a little short on local knowledge, he bought the Lewes Road land.

Mushroom culture can be very prone to fungal attack, so his first act was to import large quantities of cedar wood from his native Canada. From this timber mountain he proceeded to construct eight growing sheds, each 110ft long set out alongside each other, without windows, to help provide the best growing conditions for mushrooms to flourish. Within each shed and running for the full length 6ft wide growing beds were constructed in tiers, with ground level and raised walkways to facilitate planting, cultivation and harvesting. This layout allowed the essential process of crop rotation to take place, with every two weeks one shed being emptied, ready to start the procedure again. It would be five to six weeks before the first flush was ready for picking, and another ten to fourteen days for the next, and so on for up to about eight weeks.

In those early days it was found that the best growing medium was a good 6" layer of rotted stable manure, topped with a 1" layer of virgin top soil, the latter being steam sterilised to kill off any impurities. Fortunately stable manure was plentiful, for each shed had an extraordinary appetite of needing 32 tons at every changeover.

Labour being relatively cheap and plentiful, and the age of mechanisation in rural pursuits yet to dawn, to get the growing medium just right for cultivation was, quite literally, a hands-on job. Loads of fresh stable manure would arrive which had to be off-loaded and then turned over and over by a couple of strapping young men wielding long handled pitchforks. This was done under three 90ft x 33ft open sided sheds, which during the winter months were cold and draughty, although a good strong breeze wafting through on a hot summer's day was no doubt appreciated by the operatives.

It was after the continuous turning process had reached a considered state of readiness that a cursory inspection involving three of the five senses were employed. A good look to confirm that the texture appeared about right, next it was 'hands-on' to rifle through the pile with bare hands to make certain that the breakdown had reached the desirable state, and finally a good sniff to ensure that no traces of ammonia remained. Further, more scientific tests would be carried out before the growing compost could be spread, for if there were any virus or competitive fungus found, the whole shed would need to be steam cleaned to a very high temperature.

The harvesting was mostly carried out by women, working part-time with secondary grading taking place prior to weighing and packing into wooden or cardboard boxes before being taken to Haywards Heath station for onward transport to Victoria, where the consignment would be collected and taken to Covent Garden Market. At its peak it was quite usual for one thousand pounds in weight of mushrooms to be despatched from Lindfield in this manner every day.

Change of ownership dates have not been possible to ascertain, but Mr Slack sold out to a Mr Arthur Sparks who at the time ran a tomato nursery near Worthing.

Another change of ownership came in 1948. The Filmer family, whose father had founded a successful business in London in about 1840 manufacturing cardboard boxes, received a report from one of their representatives that Lindfield Mushroom Nursery was coming on the market. This proved of interest to the Filmer family, they made the purchase and installed their representative, Mr Gus Atkinson as Manager, a position he held until 1961.

In the meantime, the paper giant, A. E. Reed had expressed an interest in acquiring the Filmer cardboard box business, and the brothers John, Leslie and Geoffrey bought land around the mushroom factory, including Old Place Farm, Hangmans Acre and Little Walstead Farm, but Jack was retained as a consultant by Reed until he took over running the mushroom business in 1962.

Although not qualified engineers, John and his father Jack liked nothing better than tinkering with machinery and they quickly set about adapting and improving a variety of mechanical aids to remove many of the back-breaking production procedures.

Post war, stable manure was less plentiful, although experiments were successfully made with other growing materials; it was the change in labour ambitions and the consequent availability that signalled the end of the business and release of the land for housing.

In August 1915 these men, stationed in Lindfield, marched off to embark on H.M. Royal Edward bound for Gallipoli. En route the troopship was sunk by a German torpedo and of the 1400 officers and men on board, over 850 lost their lives.

Between 1914 and 1918, Lindfield was home to many army detachments, mostly cavalry and infantry. This photograph shows soldiers taking a breather having parked their 60lb field gun and tracked-vehicle in the High Street.

Priory Cottage was adapted to provide the Royal Medical Corps with a convalescent hospital during the Second World War. Those admitted wore a blue uniform with red tie to indicate that they had been wounded in combat. The lower photograph shows some of these men relaxing in the garden recovering from their injuries.

The names of ninety-five local men who gave their lives during the two World Wars are engraved on the village War Memorial. Residents in their hundreds gathered to witness the unveiling and dedication of the Memorial on 12th May 1922.

The eleventh hour, on the eleventh day, of the eleventh month and crowds gathered in front of the War Memorial in 1923 to remember those who made the supreme sacrifice.

The welcome home of soldiers, sailors and airmen who had survived the horrors of the war started with a Service of Thanksgiving, then a parade from the Church led by the Ardingly Band playing 'Sons of the Brave'. On arriving at King Edward Hall, ladies of the village had prepared a sumptuous tea and entertainment.

Full regalia and their giant and ornate banner was the order of the day as members of the South Eastern Equitable Friendly Society gathered on Lindfield Common in preparation for the 1911 local hospital parade.

c1920, and members of The Motor Mission from Newick assemble on the Common.

1921 was a good year, a very good year, for sport at Lindfield School. Having won the County Divisional Cup for cricket, the football team went on to defeat Turners Hill 3-nil to win the County Football Cup. A crowd of over 1000 lined the High Street to give the triumphant lads a cheer as they returned in their charabanc, cup held high for all to see.

This photograph can be dated to between 1902 and 1916 from two clues, it was between the time that the telegraph pole was erected and the later date when the Tiger ceased to be an inn.

It is almost a tradition that royal and certain other events on the common should include an Open Air Service. The Coronation celebrations of 1937 were no exception. The Service has been conducted from a variety of improvised platforms, including this cart with Rev. Swann leading the Prayers.

Between the wars, the village Dramatic Club annually presented in King Edward Hall a lavish production of a Gilbert and Sullivan opera. This 1934 production of 'The Mikado' featured in the 'dramatis personae' a cast of eleven principal singers, a chorus of twenty, and seventeen musicians in the orchestra.

Paxhill was built in 1595 by Ninien Boord whose father had been Court Jester to Henry VIII. During the war hundreds of Canadian troops were billeted in huts within the grounds. Just prior to 'D' Day they received visits from the King and General Montgomery.

Photographers and artists have a delicate choice to make in portraying this corner of Lindfield, should it be from the north or south? Most play safe by opting for both. Little wonder that the finished work is often titled 'A pretty corner of Lindfield'.

Photographs of Old Place and Thatched Cottage are so numerous that it was difficult to choose just one for inclusion. This view is believed to be one of the oldest in existence. A hunting lodge to Henry VII, Thatched Cottage has also served as a poor house. Old Place was the home of Charles Kempe, the Victorian stained glass expert.

It is a pity that the writing on the hanging sign cannot be deciphered, but it does give credence that Grange Farm at the foot of Town Hill was once a hostelry called The Crawford Arms.

In 1904 the tennis courts on the common were moved to the position shown in this picture, near to Burnt House Farm. However, by the 1930s, the Bowling Club were desperate for more room and the Tennis Club agreed to vacate in favour of where they now are, and were previously.

A stagnant pond surrounded by a rickety fence is hardly an inspiring prospect for a bowling green, but in 1904 that was the intention of club members. They took off their coats and physically set to drain, level and turf the site. In a few short months they had transformed this corner of the common.

Those magnificent men in their flying machines came to Lindfield on 22nd April 1922. A training flight of H.M. Airship Gamma made a scheduled landing on the common, out stepped Capt. P. Broke-Smith who led his fellow officers on a walk up to Lindfield House to take breakfast with his father-in-law, Admiral Twiss at Lindfield House.

A horse drinking-trough had been installed on the common as a permanent commemoration of the Coronation of King George V in 1911, now 25 years later, on 5th May 1935, crowds gathered to witness Mrs Cumberlege unveil a new village sign to mark the Royal Jubilee.

A group of local fruit pickers pose for this photograph in the gardens of Snowflakes, Mr Holmans property in Walstead.

The village contingent of The Church Lads Brigade on parade Easter Sunday 1911.

Two photographs taken at opposite ends of the war. Even before Prime Minister Neville Chamberlain had announced on 3rd September 1939 that we were at war with Germany, evacuee children from London started to arrive in Lindfield. The Germans having been defeated in May 1945 was the time when local lads built this bonfire to celebrate the end of six long war years, although hostilities in the Far East would continue until August.

The first part of Lewes Road nearest the Post Office was originally called Kent Street, and here can be seen Frederick Cottages to the right, and Carriers on the left. The cottages further on and the weatherboard building have been demolished to make way for The Evangelical Free Church in Chaloner Road.

Rowstile was a two-barred stile next to a single plank of wood bridging a stream leading to meadows from where the tennis courts are now situated. Nearby were Lindfield Cottages, built in 1881 and in use until at least 1935. The site was then added to the common.

These houses in West View have enviable views across the common and the many activities that take place there. The Rosmond Cheese Factory was situated at the far end, but photographs of it appear to be non-existent.

These twelve houses were the first and for a very long time the only houses in Eastern Road. At the junction with Luxford Road was a copse, referred to as the Plantation, which made a wonderful adventure playground for imaginative children.

Cricket has been played on Lindfield common for over 250 years. This photograph of a Lindfield team is probably one of the oldest in existence being c1890.

Just ten years after taking off their jackets to create a bowling green from scratch, these members in 1914 had every justification for posing proudly before their thatched roof pavilion.

In 1921, this Lindfield football team beat Wivelsfield 21 goals to nil, with every member of the team putting the ball in the back of the net. This included the goalkeeper who scored from a penalty kick.

Stoolball is not unique to, but very closely associated with Sussex, and is believed to be one of the oldest games played in the United Kingdom. This photograph is of the Lindfield School team of 1927.

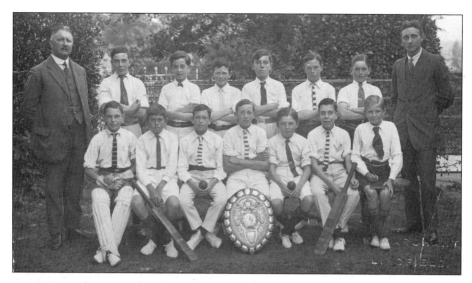

The 1921 Lindfield Junior School had every right to pose proudly displaying their trophies. This was the year that the school won both the County Cups in football and cricket and it is probable that some boys played in both teams.

Tug of war matches always appear to be something of impromptu events, a group of heavies from the pubs and clubs coming forward to out-heave each other at fetes and common events. This is the winning team on Jubilee Day 1935.

A mixed class of 1917 at the Lewes Road school sit attentively at their desks for the photograph.

This school group photograph of 1908 is a superb example of Lindfield Remembered, it includes a young Mrs Lucy Baird in the dark dress, second from the right, front row. Mrs Baird is now 104.

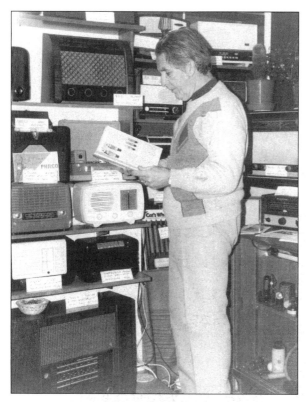

Following retirement in 1988, Ray Leworthy assembled his extensive collection of 'steam' wirelesses and associated components and established a Wireless Museum and Workshop in one of the old Durrant brewery buildings to the rear of The Linden Tree. Health problems forced Ray to give up his interests in 1999.

Surrounded for many years by temporary classrooms, this photograph gives a glimpse of the Reading Rooms, or Social Centre, in Lewes Road with members of The Church Lads Brigade, 1904.

Fred Tate (1867-1943) played for Lindfield Cricket Club and was a member of the club committee. Between 1888 and 1905 he played for Sussex, and when chosen to play for England in the fourth Test Match at Old Trafford, which coincided with his 35th birthday, it was to end in personal misfortune, when he dropped a crucial catch from the Australian captain in the second innings. Joe Donlevy, the Aussie captain went on to score 37 out of his team's total of 186. This left England needing only eight runs to win when Fred Tate came in to bat at number 11; he scored a four, but was then bowled out, the last man. Australia won by three runs and took the Ashes.

Tate was so distraught that he cried in the dressing-room and his anguish persisted on the journey home on the train. He was so disconsolate that on arriving home he, on viewing this photograph of himself with his five year old son Maurice, hoped fervently that Tate Junior would, in due course, make amends for his father's inauspicious performance. Maurice Tate (1895-1956) played for England 39 times and in 20 consecutive Test Matches against Australia. His distinguished cricketing career with Sussex and England more than atoned for his father's Old Trafford disappointment, and although the father was selected to play for his country but once, they remain the only father and son to represent England against Australia.

PETER DUNCAN. Born Chelsea 1947, moved with his parents to Lindfield in 1960. After several years as a qualified journeyman in the printing trade, joined his father's signwriting business, continuing with this since his father's death and this remains his main source of employment. Started collecting old postcards in the late 1980s and spends many weekends attending collectors' fairs, allowing him to amass a substantial collection of locally related postcards. Married to Jenny Holman from Walstead, they have two sons.

GWYN MANSFIELD. A Kentish Man by birth, born in Gravesend 1927. Moved to Lindfield 1983. Co-opted member Lindfield Parish Council 1992/1996. Initiated and produced the *Village Directory & Year Book 1993/2000*, with Claudia Gaukroger published *Lindfield Within Living Memory* 1995, established the Lindfield Archive Collection 1996, organised the schools Scrap Book competition and *The Lindfield Times for the Millennium,* and acted as co-ordinator for the Lindfield Millennium Map project.

BRIAN TESTER. A life-long Lindfield resident whose family have lived in the village for over 150 years. A former pupil of the Lindfield Lewes Road School, he subsequently became a Governor of the school. He is a past Chairman of The King Edward Hall Management Committee and was co-Chairman of the Lindfield Silver Jubilee celebrations in 1977. He is now a locally-based Chartered Surveyor and Construction Consultant. He has contributed to a number of publications illustrated with pictures from his collection of historic photographs and postcards.

↚ AUTHORS' NOTES ↛

Most of the illustrations in this book are from the authors' joint collections built up over a period of many years and from a wide variety of sources. It has been impossible to remember the name of everyone who has contributed, but we would like to thank them in absentia, and to record our thanks to those of more recent years whose names come to mind and who have helped to bring variety to the illustrations - Derek Bacon, Mary Botting, Norman Burtenshaw, Patricia Calderwood, Dave Cooper, Rodney Durrant, John Filmer, Claude Ferguson, Gillian Harrison, Robert Humphreys, Neil Kerslake, Jerry Masters, Harold Mighall, Daisy Philpott, Dick Rawlings, Pete Richards, Eileen Roles, Nickola Smith, Myrtle Stenton, Dave Tucker, David Shepherd and Stanley Walder.

Thanks are also acknowledged of help from The Lindfield Archive Collection.

The laws of copyright are complex and a great deal of effort has gone into ensuring that there has been no infringement. We apologise if there has been any inadvertent lapse on our part.

Time can play havoc with memories and it is possible that when checking the veracity of captions and story lines there can be slight variances to other persons' recall.

Enlarged, mounted copies of many of the photographs included in this book, plus others, may be purchased from Peter Duncan, 'Postcards from the Past', 22 The Welkin, Lindfield. Tel: 01444 482620, mobile: 07790 720239.